The Anger Book

A Journal To Destroy

Impressum
© 2023 Independently published by Elias Baar
Bärenstraße 1, 73035 Göppingen
Germany

ISBN: 9798389850095

Cover design by Andrew Back

THIS JOURNAL BELONGS TO:

_____

WHAT THIS BOOK IS ABOUT

anger is a natural emotion that we all experience at some point in our lives. it can be a powerful force that drives us to take action and make changes in our lives, but it can also be destructive if not properly managed. *the anger book* is designed to help readers understand the underlying causes of their anger as well as encouraging readers to use writing as a tool for managing their anger rather than lashing out or making impulsive decisions in the heat of the moment.

the anger book is a source of support for those who feel alone in their struggles with anger. by putting their anger on paper, readers can gain a better understanding of the root causes of their emotions and begin to develop healthier coping mechanisms. the act of writing can also serve as a form of catharsis, allowing readers to release their frustrations and gain a sense of clarity.

in essence, *the anger book* serves as a safe space for readers to rant about everything that's been bothering them without fear of judgment or consequences. through writing, readers can learn to manage their anger in a constructive and healthy way, ultimately leading to a more fulfilling and satisfying life.

5 reasons for *the anger book*

1 – it helps you to control your emotions

letting out anger on paper can help reduce stress and tension in your body, leading to improved mental and emotional well-being. holding onto anger and repressing it can lead to chronic stress and negative effects on mental health, whereas expressing anger can help you process it and move on. *releasing anger in a healthy way can help prevent feelings of resentment and bitterness from building up, leading to improved mental clarity and a more positive outlook on life.*

2 – it's built on psychology

studies have shown that journaling can help *reduce symptoms of anger, depression and trauma.* it can help you organizing your thoughts, expressing yourself and dealing with your emotions, both good and bad, in a positive, healthy way.

3 – it's a journal for people who don't know what to journal about

if you're that kind of person who wants to get into journaling, but doesn't know when or what to write about, look no further. *the anger book is a guided journal to help improve your mental health, designed for you.*

4 – self-reflection is the road toward healing

through self-discovery, we can find who we are and whom we want to be. divided into three chapters, *the anger book* allows you to recognize & acknowledge your deepest emotions, invites you to step inside yourself, and ultimately helps you gain clarity in your mind.

5 – this journal is just for you

writing your thoughts and feelings down in a journal allows you to craft and maintain your sense of self and solidifies your identity. the trick is to keep exploring yourself. *close your door when you open this book. breath, flip through the pages and be completely honest with yourself.*

WHENEVER YOU ARE FEELING

ANGRY,

JEALOUS,

FRUSTRATED,

ANNOYED,

MAD,

TRAPPED,

IRRITATED,

WHENEVER YOU ARE FEELING ANY EMOTIONS
OF ANGER,

WHENEVER YOUR BRAIN CAN'T SHUT UP,

THINK ABOUT THIS BOOK.

HOW THIS BOOK WORKS:

1. WRITE IT ALL DOWN
2. RIP IT OUT
3. DESTROY IT

WHY DESTROY IT*

writing down negative and unwanted thoughts, and then ripping them out, can be a helpful practice for us to mentally discard those thoughts. this process can provide a sense of finality to these negative thoughts and can trick the brain into marking them as gone instead of suppressing them. our neural circuitry does not always differentiate between the mental and physical, which is why physically discarding negative thoughts can turn down their mental volume. this technique provides a simple yet effective way for us to cope with angry thoughts and move on from them.

CONTENTS

chapter one: *letting it all out*

the first step in releasing anger is to let it all out. this means expressing your feelings in a healthy and constructive way. a journal is a great tool to use for this because you can write down all your thoughts and emotions without worrying about being judged or holding back. write down everything that you're feeling, no matter how intense or irrational it may seem. don't censor yourself. just let it all out on the page.

chapter two: *calming down*

once you've expressed your anger in your journal, it's time to calm down and heal. there are several ways to do this, but some of the most effective include deep breathing exercises, mindfulness meditation, and realizing that it's okay to feel how you feel. the key is to focus on your body and mind and to bring them into a state of calm. this will help you to see your anger from a new perspective and to start processing it in a healthier way. you are not alone.

chapter three: *growing from your anger*

the final step in releasing anger is to grow from it. this means learning from your experiences and making positive changes in your life. look back and reflect on what caused your anger and what you can do to prevent similar situations in the future. think about what you can do to be more assertive, to communicate more effectively, or to cope with anger in a healthier way.

letting go

*anger is not just an aggressive reaction. it often provides
us with information that allows us to better engage with
the world around us (as well as ourselves). if we see anger
as something that makes us more informed, we can adapt
our response accordingly to better our position. those
prompts are an invitation to realize & acknowledge your
deepest emotions. take a deep breath. be honest about your
thoughts and feelings, then rip it out and destroy it.*

A LETTER TO MY ANGER:

DESTROY THIS PAGE!

WRITE A LETTER TO SOMEONE WHO HURT YOU:

RIP THIS PAGE OUT AND DESTROY IT!

PAINT YOUR FEELING:

AND THEN PAINT OVER IT.

AND OVER IT.

WHAT EMOTIONS, THOUGHTS OR EXPERIENCES FEEL HEAVY RIGHT NOW?

DESTROY THIS PAGE!

WHAT ARE YOU HOLDING ONTO THAT IS STILL HURTING YOU?

LET GO AND DESTROY THIS PAGE!

I AM JEALOUS OF:

DESTROY THIS PAGE!

WRITE A LETTER TO A PERSON WHO HURT YOU:

RIP THIS PAGE OUT AND NEVER SEND IT!

VENT TO ME:

35

AND THEN DESTROY THIS PAGE!

I WILL NEVER FORGIVE MY PARENTS FOR THIS:

BURN THIS PAGE!

WHAT'S SOMETHING YOU WISH YOU HAD SAID?

DESTROY THIS PAGE!

FIND A CREATIVE WAY TO DESTROY THIS PAGE!

WRITE DOWN THE THOUGHTS YOU'RE TOO
SCARED TO LOOK AT:

AND THEN PAINT OVER IT WITH BLACK LIKE IT
WAS NEVER THERE!

THE APOLOGY I WOULD LIKE TO RECEIVE:

DESTROY THIS PAGE!

THINGS I COULDN'T SAY TO MY PARENTS:

DESTROY THIS PAGE!

WRITE ABOUT A CHILDHOOD MEMORY THAT
BRINGS YOU THE MOST SORROW. WRITE AS IF
YOU WERE A CHILD, JUST LIKE THE CHILD THAT
STILL LIVES WITHIN YOU.

PAINT OVER THIS PAGE.

PAINT LIKE A CHILD.

WHAT OR WHO DO YOU NEED TO LET GO OF?

WHY?

LET GO BY DESTROYING THIS PAGE!

WHAT ARE YOU HOLDING ONTO THAT'S STILL HURTING YOU?

DESTROY THIS PAGE!

WHAT'S THE MOST PAINFUL THING YOU'VE BEEN TOLD?

THAT'S NOT TRUE. NOW DESTROY THIS PAGE!

THE EXACT WORDS THAT COMPLETELY
DESTROYED ME:

DESTROY THIS PAGE!

THINGS I SAID OUT OF ANGER THAT I REGRET:

DESTROY THIS PAGE!

HARDEST DECISION I HAD TO MAKE:

DESTROY THIS PAGE!

THINGS MY PARENTS NEVER PRAISED ME FOR:

I AM PROUD OF YOU.

YOU DESERVE BETTER.

THINGS I REGRET:

DESTROY THIS PAGE!

HOW I FEEL ABOUT MYSELF:

DESTROY THIS PAGE!

A FEELING I'LL NEVER FORGET:

DESTROY THIS PAGE!

SOMETHING I CAN'T SAY OUT LOUD:

DESTROY THIS PAGE BEOFRE SOMEONE SEES IT!

THIS FEELS HARD TO LOVE ABOUT MYSELF:

DESTROY THIS!

I AM ANGRY BECAUSE OF:

DESTROY THIS PAGE!

THINGS I HATE:

NOW DESTROY THIS PAGE!

CUT THIS PAGE INTO 100 PIECES!

healing

"healing" is a modest compilation of love letters that delve
into the deep-seated themes of sorrow, relinquishment,
self-love, and hopeful growth. these love letters provide a
cathartic experience for those who struggle with anger,
allowing them to confront their tumultuous emotions
head-on. the poignant words of each letter offer a sense of
solace and serve as a reminder that healing from anger can
be a challenging process, but it is possible with patience,
perseverance, and a commitment to self-awareness.

i hope you know it's okay that you don't have it all figured out yet, because life is a journey and not a destination. it's a journey filled with ups and downs, twists and turns, and sometimes it can be a little messy. but that's what makes life so beautiful, so unpredictable, and so worth living. so don't be too hard on yourself, and remember that it's okay to make mistakes, it's okay to change your mind, and it's okay to not have everything figured out. embrace the journey and enjoy the ride.

believe in yourself and trust the journey life has taken you on. every year is a chance to grow and start anew, to face the world with confidence and live the life you desire. don't let fear hold you back, whether it's fear of failure, heartbreak or falling. these fears exist only in your mind and dwelling on them will only lead to regret. overthinking can be a self-sabotaging act, causing doubt in yourself and leading to a loss of identity. but i know you're stronger than that, you're capable of overcoming and achieving great things. believe in yourself and keep moving forward.

anger can often be a manifestation of fear. when we feel threatened or in danger, our body's natural response is to either fight or flee. anger is a way of fighting back, either through verbal or physical means. fear triggers the release of stress hormones, such as cortisol and adrenaline, which can lead to an increased heart rate, rapid breathing, and muscle tension - all of which are also characteristic of anger. therefore, it is important for us to understand that anger is just a symptom of fear and to address the underlying fear or insecurity in order to effectively manage and control anger. by doing so, we can learn to respond to triggering situations with a sense of calmness and rationality rather than reacting impulsively with anger.

it's time to let go of all that worrying and have faith in life's path. every new year brings with it growth and the chance to bloom again. embrace every moment, big or small, with open arms and don't be afraid to take risks and chase your dreams. overthinking can be a heavy burden, but you are braver and stronger than it. don't let doubts and fears weigh you down. you are capable of so much more and always deserve to be happy.

you deserve to be happy, fully and completely. your journey through life has been filled with challenges and triumphs, hardships and joys, and through it all, you have shown immense strength and resilience. your laughter, your kindness, your passions and dreams are what make you truly special and deserving of happiness. don't let anyone or anything dim your light or make you question your worth. you are worthy and deserving of all the love, peace, and happiness this world has to offer. so hold your head up high and keep shining. you got this.

it is a beautiful truth that what is truly meant for us will always stay with us, no matter what challenges we face or how far we wander. whether it be a person who brings love and laughter into our lives, a dream that ignites our passions, or a journey that shapes us into who we are meant to be, everything that is meant to be a part of our story will never leave our side. it is important to remember this, especially in the face of uncertainty or loss. trust in the journey and have faith in yourself, for you possess the strength and resilience to overcome any obstacle and attract everything you need to fulfill your destiny. so hold onto this truth and never let it go – what is meant for you will always be yours, now and forever.

you are allowed to feel angry about what has happened, while also having hope that just because the situation cannot be changed or erased, that does not mean you cannot have a beautiful future that will be meaningful and special in its own way. you might not be able to forgive those who have wronged you in the same way you forgave others, but you can still find peace within yourself. you might not be able to control the external circumstances that caused your anger, but you can still choose to let go of the negative emotions and move forward with positivity. yes, the present moment may be difficult and different from the past, but perhaps, that can be a beautiful thing.

it hurts to let go of something that once brought us so much happiness, but sometimes it's necessary for our own growth and well-being. our needs, desires, and goals change over time, and if a relationship no longer aligns with who we are or where we want to go, it may be time to say goodbye. this doesn't mean the love was never real, but rather that it has served its purpose and it's time to move forward. holding onto what was will only hold us back from finding what is meant to be.

it's natural to feel anger in response to injustices or challenges we face, but we must remember to channel that energy in a positive direction. instead of allowing anger to turn into bitterness, we can use it as fuel for action. we can write about it, paint it, dance it, and use our voices to speak out about the issues that matter to us. by doing so, we can effect change and make a positive impact on the world around us. so let's harness our anger in a constructive way, and never stop working towards a better future for ourselves and those around us.

you deserve to be loved the way you love others, with an open heart and unwavering devotion. your kind and compassionate spirit should be met with equal kindness and compassion. don't settle for anything less, for you are deserving of the love you give so freely. embrace the love you have for others and allow yourself to be loved in the same way, with no bounds or restrictions. you are worthy of this love, so don't hesitate to seek it out and bask in its warmth.

healing is a journey, not a destination. it takes time, patience, and compassion, both for oneself and others. it requires us to confront our pain, acknowledge our wounds, and confront our fears. but above all, healing is a choice. a choice to let go of anger, to forgive, and to embrace love. it is a journey that leads us from darkness to light, from brokenness to wholeness, and from hatred to peace.

i want you to remember how far you've come and how strong you've become. you should be proud of yourself for still standing, for still smiling, and for never giving up. your unwavering spirit and resilience are truly admirable and a testament to your character.

i know that life can be challenging at times, but i want you to know that you are capable of overcoming any obstacle that comes your way. your past experiences have made you stronger and better equipped to handle difficult situations. so never lose faith in yourself and always believe in your own strength and abilities.

i want you to know that better days are ahead, just like the sun rises after a stormy night. hold your head up high, and keep pushing forward, for a brighter tomorrow awaits you. you got this.

i admire your bravery. waking up each day with a heavy heart and facing a messy life is not easy, but you still manage to be resilient and not let the world dim your spirit. your ability to continue to love, express and be vulnerable, despite past experiences, shows your inner strength. your persistence in believing in something greater and keeping a positive outlook, even when uncertain, is commendable. your daily fight and determination to move forward only makes you stronger and i truly believe that is what defines your true strength.

in a world filled with anger and hate, it can be tempting to give into those negative emotions. but i encourage you to resist that urge and instead strive to cultivate kindness and understanding. it's important to acknowledge your anger and frustrations, but it's equally important to not let them consume you. keep trying to see the good in others, even when it's difficult. remember, hate only brings more hate. so instead, choose to spread love and positivity, and do your part in creating a more peaceful world. keep pushing forward, even when it feels like the world is against you. you got this.

in case no one has told you this lately: the love you offer to others is the same love you deserve for yourself. you are important, not just for what you can do for others, but for simply being alive and breathing. you deserve to find your place in the world and to be fully present in your own life. just as you appreciate the beauty and stories of those around you, know that your own story and experiences are also valuable and worth sharing. you have a loving heart and a keen eye for goodness in the world. so, may you never doubt that you are deserving of the same love and kindness that you pour out onto others.

it is normal to feel sad or overwhelmed at times, but it's important not to dwell on those feelings. instead, make an effort to focus on the good things in life. the simple moments of happiness, the small acts of kindness, and the little victories. they may seem insignificant, but they bring us so much joy and make life worth living. of course, it's okay to feel bad sometimes, but it's crucial not to give up. use those moments as an opportunity to grow and learn, and don't be afraid to reach out for help if you need it. remember, it's not about being happy all the time, it's about finding joy in the journey, no matter what obstacles you may face. so keep your head up and never give up on yourself.

anger is often perceived as a negative emotion, but when channeled properly, it can be a powerful force for good. it can drive us to fight for what we believe in, to stand up for ourselves and those around us, and to push for positive change in the world. but it's important to remember that anger should never be used as a means to harm others. instead, use it as a motivator to bring about positive growth and progress in your own life and in the lives of those around you. when used in a constructive manner, anger can be a powerful tool that helps us to overcome obstacles, pursue our passions, and create a better world for all. so, embrace your anger, but channel it towards positive change and never let it control you.

you're going to get hurt again, but don't let that stop you from opening your heart. the fear of being hurt again is understandable, but it shouldn't hold you back from experiencing the joys of love and connection. every relationship, whether it be romantic or platonic, involves a certain level of vulnerability and the possibility of getting hurt. but the beauty of life lies in taking risks, in putting yourself out there and allowing yourself to love and be loved. the pain of a past hurt may linger, but it should not define or limit your future experiences. embrace the journey, learn from the past and trust that the love you give and receive will be worth the risk. the pain is just a reminder of how much you've truly loved and the memories and growth that came with it.

some days will feel harder than others but remember that even the toughest days are just temporary. don't give up, don't give in to the negative thoughts and feelings. keep pushing forward, stay strong and have faith in the journey. every obstacle, every challenge, every hard day is just a step in the growth process. and just like the night always gives way to the morning, these tough times will eventually come to an end. the sun will always rise again, and brighter days are ahead. so hold on and never lose hope in the journey of your life.

never let the struggles of life dull your spark of kindness. never let the hardships of life dim your shining spirit of kindness. your compassion, empathy, and generosity are some of your greatest strengths, and they have the power to brighten the darkest of days for those around you. when you give of yourself, you not only bring joy to others, but you also bring more positivity and happiness into your own life. hold onto your kindness, let it guide your actions and inspire those around you. your kindness has the power to make a difference and will leave a lasting impact on the world.

right now, focus on yourself. invest in your own growth, well-being, and happiness. the world will still be there when you're ready, but for now, prioritize taking care of yourself. explore your passions, cultivate new interests, and challenge yourself to learn and grow. surround yourself with positivity, eliminate toxic relationships, and invest in meaningful connections with those who bring joy to your life. remember, you can only pour from an overflowing cup, so take care of yourself first. the world will still be there when you're ready, but for now, give yourself the gift of self-care and focus on becoming the best version of yourself. you deserve it.

there's no such thing as the right person at the wrong time. the universe has a funny way of bringing people together at the most unexpected moments, but it's up to us to recognize the significance and make the most of it. love is a powerful force that transcends all boundaries, including time. it has the ability to heal wounds, mend broken hearts, and create a bond that lasts a lifetime. so, don't let the fear of timing hold you back from pursuing the one who makes your heart skip a beat. instead, embrace the opportunity, take a leap of faith, and trust that everything will fall into place.

the truth is, love exists in so much more than just romantic relationships. it's the gentle touch of a mother's hand, the memories shared with a cherished pet, the warm smile from a stranger. love can be found in the simplest of moments, in the embrace of family, in the selfless acts of kindness. it has the power to heal wounds, mend broken hearts, and bring light into the darkest of days. love is what makes life worth living and it's a journey we should all embrace with open hearts. so, let's cherish the love we have in our lives, be grateful for the love we receive, and continue to spread love wherever we go. for it is through love that we truly find meaning, happiness and fulfillment.

i understand that you may not believe me when i say that you'll be okay, as you might think no one understands your pain or cannot empathize with you. but i want you to know that these thoughts are not true. instead, let me tell you this: you will get through today, one step at a time. by simply taking breaths, putting one foot in front of the other, and making even the slightest progress, you will make it to bedtime tonight with a sense of accomplishment for facing the day and yourself. with each passing day, the journey will become easier, the mornings less heavy, and your heart lighter. in time, you will heal and find wholeness again.

i hope you have the courage to see endings in a positive light as opportunities for growth and transformation. i hope you have the courage to let love and new opportunities flow into your life like rain, without trying to control or change them. i hope you have the courage to accept people and circumstances for what they are, and to view endings as the building blocks of the chapters in your life that have changed you, without feeling like they have to be a part of your future. and when you've reached that point, i hope you have the courage to give yourself the closure you need. to be your own safe haven and find peace within yourself. i hope you have the courage to not let the losses define you, to not let them burrow into the core of your being and convince you that you have failed or that you are not worthy of happiness. i hope you have the courage to see the love, effort, and fight you put in as a testament to the depth of your emotions and the beauty of life's moments. and most of all, i hope you have the courage to move forward.

the hardest thing you have to do in life is to let go of people you wanted in your life forever. letting go of someone you wanted in your life forever is not an easy task, but it's a testament to the depth of your love and the strength you possess. i know it can be difficult to accept that this person may not be a part of your future, but it's a crucial step towards growth and healing. holding on to what could have been will only hold you back from finding new happiness. i understand that letting go brings feelings of emptiness and uncertainty, but it also opens up the door for new love and opportunities to come into your life. so, be kind to yourself and trust that everything will work out in the end. letting go does not mean you have lost a part of yourself; it simply means that you have made room for new growth and experiences. i believe in you.

you are enough, just as you are, with all your flaws and imperfections. don't let anyone tell you otherwise. your journey through life is one-of-a-kind and valuable, and it's shaped by your experiences and perspectives. don't be afraid to be yourself and embrace your individuality. embrace the things that make you unique, even if they don't conform to society's standards. remember that you are loved and appreciated for who you are, and that your presence in this world has a purpose. keep striving to be the best version of yourself, but never forget that you are enough just as you are.

it took me a while to understand that not all events in life have to have a picturesque outcome. not everyone we form a strong connection with is destined to become a permanent fixture in our lives. some people come into our lives to educate us on how to love and others come to instruct us on how not to love, how to avoid settling, and how to never compromise ourselves again. while it can be painful when people leave, their teachings endure and that is what counts. that is what stays with us.

instead of trying to handle someone who is not prepared to be with you, walk away. cherish yourself and leave anyone who fails to recognize your value. eventually, you will encounter someone who will fully appreciate your greatness, making you question why you ever spent time with someone who didn't understand your worth. regardless of how good it may seem, walk away from anyone who is indecisive about you. if they were truly right for you, you wouldn't be constantly worrying about the reasons why you two aren't together.

i hope you find what you're truly searching for, and that what you find is happiness. may your journey towards it be filled with moments of joy, laughter, and love. may you discover that happiness is not just a destination, but a state of mind and a choice you make every day. may you find it in the small things, in the people who bring light to your life, and in the memories you create along the way. i wish you the courage to pursue your passions, the wisdom to navigate life's challenges, and the grace to accept and embrace every experience, good or bad, as a precious opportunity for growth and self-discovery. i hope you find what you're looking for, and may it be more than you ever imagined.

growing

anger shows you what you're passionate about, where your boundaries are, and what you believe needs to change about the world. those prompts are an invitation to step inside yourself. take a deep breath. flip through the book, stop on one page and write your heart out. those are questions to keep.

describe a situation that made you extremely angry.

what triggered your anger and how did you react?

keep this.

reflect on a time when you expressed your anger in a way
that you now regret.

what would you have done differently?

keep this.

write about a person who consistently makes you angry. how do they make you feel and what steps can you take to manage your reactions towards them?

keep this.

how have your past mistakes shaped the person you are today?

keep this.

what are the qualities and traits that make you unique and valuable?

keep this.

write about a time when your anger affected your relationships. how did you resolve the situation and what did you learn from it?

keep this.

how do you typically cope with your anger? are there any
unhealthy coping mechanisms you want to work on
changing?

keep this.

think about a situation where you forgave someone who made you angry. what led to your decision to forgive and how did it impact your emotions?

keep this.

write about a situation where you channeled your anger into something productive. what did you do and how did it make you feel?

keep this.

who makes you feel loved when you don't feel lovable?

keep this.

write a letter to someone who has made you feel angry, expressing your emotions and thoughts without sending it.

keep this.

you've made it through every bad day so far. you can make it through this. what is hard on you right now?

keep this.

what did your last relationship teach you about yourself?

keep this.

who are you with when you feel your best?

keep this.

write down all the things that make you feel calm and peaceful and create a plan for incorporating them into your daily routine.

keep and remember this.

what is something you hide from others that you are proud of?

keep this.

what is your favorite thing about yourself?

keep this.

what makes you feel close to yourself?

keep this.

what is something you accomplished recently that you're proud of?

keep this.

what are some limiting beliefs or negative self-talk patterns you have? write down positive affirmations to counteract negative thoughts that lead to anger, such as "i am in control of my emotions" or "i choose to react with kindness and understanding."

keep this.

what is something you want to forgive yourself for? how can you offer yourself the same kindness and understanding that you would to a friend?

keep this.

what is something you've learned about yourself recently?
how can you use that knowledge to better support and care
for yourself?

keep this.

what scares you, but is worth doing anyway?

keep this.

what is something you're grateful for today?

keep this.

if you could forgive someone who hurt you in the past,
how would that change your life?

keep this.

what are you still trying to prove to yourself?

keep this.

list three things you're grateful for today and why they
bring you joy.

keep this.

consider what your future self would want you to know
and do to heal and let go of the past. write a letter to
yourself as if you were writing to a friend.

keep this.

reflect on the ways in which your past experiences have shaped you into the person you are today. write down the lessons you have learned and the strengths you have gained.

keep this.

reflect on the ways in which your anger has impacted the people around you and write down steps for repairing any relationships that may have been damaged.

keep this.

reflect on the impact that your thoughts and emotions have on your life and write down steps for cultivating a positive and mindful outlook.

keep this.

thank you for trusting me and this journal.

tag us in your story on instagram @modernframeofmind & @elias.baar, tiktok: @thesadnessbook & @modernframeofmind, or send us an email: hello@modernfom.com

for business inquiries: elias@modernfom.com

i love you,

stay strong.

Printed in Great Britain
by Amazon

24589197R00103